WHAT IS ART?

Photography

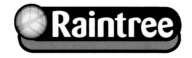

KAREN HOSACK

www.raintreepublishers.co.uk
Visit our website to find out more information about Raintree books.

To order:
☎ Phone 44 (0) 1865 888112
▤ Send a fax to 44 (0) 1865 314091
💻 Visit the Raintree Bookshop at www.raintreepublishers.co.uk to brows
our catalogue and order online

First published in Great Britain by Raintree,
Halley Court, Jordan Hill, Oxford OX2 8EJ,
part of Pearson Education.
Raintree is a registered trademark of Pearson
Education Ltd.

© Pearson Education Ltd 2008
The moral right of the proprietor has been asserted.

Editorial: Adam Miller, Charlotte Guillain,
Clare Lewis and Catherine Veitch
Design: Victoria Bevan and AMR Design Ltd
Illustrations: David Woodroffe
Picture Research: Mica Brancic
Production: Victoria Fitzgerald

Originated by Dot Gradations Ltd, UK
Printed and bound by CTPS (China Translation
& Printing Services Ltd)

ISBN 978 1 4062 0937 2
12 11 10 09 08
10 9 8 7 6 5 4 3 2 1

British Library Cataloguing in Publication Data
Hosack, Karen
   Photography. - (What is art?)
   1. Photography - Juvenile literature 2. Photography -
   Appreciation - Juvenile literature
   I. Title
   770
A full catalogue record for this book is available from
the British Library.

Acknowledgements
The publishers would like to thank the following for
permission to reproduce photographs:
Copyright of the artist, Courtesy Anthony Reynolds
Gallery p. **7**; ©Scala, Florence p. **20** (©Man Ray
Trust/ADAGP, Paris and DACS, London 2008); The
Bridgeman Art Library pp. **10** (Gemaeldegalerie
Alte Meister, Dresden, Germany/ Staatliche
Kunstsammlungen Dresden), **21** ©The Bridgeman
Art Library, **21**(© Salvador Dali, Gala-Salvador Dali
Foundation, DACS, London 2008), **22** (Museo di Storia
della Fotografia Fratelli Alinari, Florence, Alinari), **27**
(Private Collection, Archives Charmet); ©The British
Library p. **4**; ©Corbis pp. **5** (Ansel Adams Publishing
Rights Trust), **12** (The Andy Warhol Foundation for
the Visual Arts), **15** (Joe Rosenthal); ©David Hockney
p. **8**; Digital Image © The Museum of Modern Art p.
6 (Licensed by SCALA/Art Resource, NY); with kind
permission from Ellen Ugelstad p. **9**; ©Getty pp. **15b**
(2001 The Record (Bergen Record, N.J.) Photo by
Thomas E. Franklin), **24** (TimeLife pictures/Andreas
Feininger); ©International Center of Photography (ICA)
p. **18**; ©Jeff Wall p. **19** (Tate Gallery, London, Great
Britain); ©Panos Pictures p. **17** (Georg Gerster); ©Rex
Features Ltd pp. **14**, **25**; ©Science Photo Library pp.
16 (Prof. Harold E Edgerton), **26** (Adam HartDavis);
©Sothebys p. **13**; ©Tom Hunter p. **11** (The Saatchi
Gallery); ©Tony Howell p. **23**.

Cover photograph of lemon splashing into water
reproduced with permission of Getty Images/
Photonica/VEER George Diebold.

Every effort has been made to contact copyright
holders of any material reproduced in this book.
Any omissions will be rectified in subsequent
printings if notice is given to the publishers.

Disclaimer

Contents

Any words appearing in the text in bold, **like this**,
are explained in the glossary.

Photography and art

Ever since the first camera was used in 1827, people have used photography to record many things. Some people use cameras to capture personal special events, like birthdays or weddings. **Journalists** take photographs to show moments in history.

Some artists use photography either as a tool to help them produce a final work, or as the final work itself. Here, two artists have taken photographs instead of painting a picture. The process of making the image is very different from painting.

The Haystack by William Henry Fox Talbot, c.1844

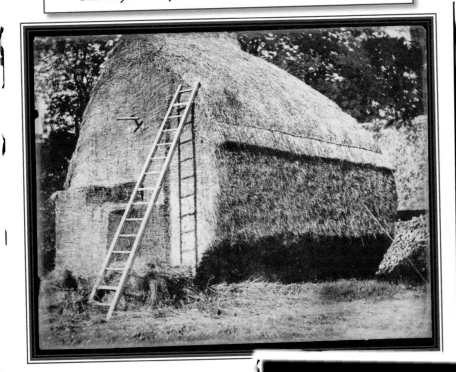

The artist has set up the scene so we think that the people building the haystack have only been gone for a short while. What clues help you to think this?

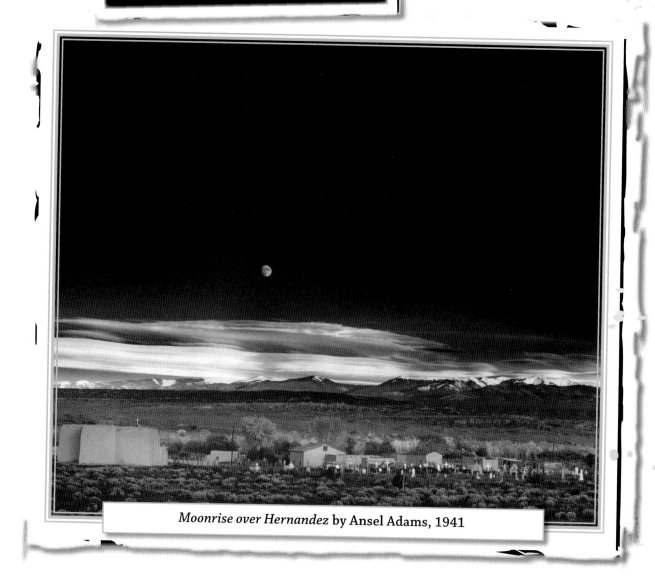

Moonrise over Hernandez by Ansel Adams, 1941

In the early photograph opposite we can see a haystack on a sunny day. We can tell that it must be summer because that's when people make hay.

This photograph of the moon rising also makes us think about how people are involved in a **landscape**. But the photograph doesn't show anyone. How has the artist done this?

5

Telling a story

What can we tell about this woman by just looking at the photograph? The photographer has spent time making sure the image is lit well. The light makes her hat and veil cast a small shadow across her face. This makes her look slightly mysterious. She wears a lot of make-up and jewellery and we can see she is sitting in a bar.

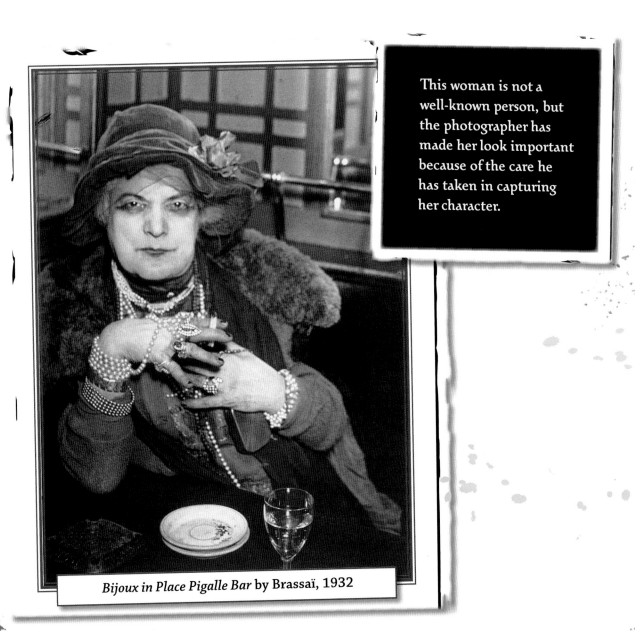

This woman is not a well-known person, but the photographer has made her look important because of the care he has taken in capturing her character.

Bijoux in Place Pigalle Bar by Brassaï, 1932

The artist who took this photograph only gives us a small amount of information to help us build a story around the character in the image. We have to make up the rest of the story ourselves.

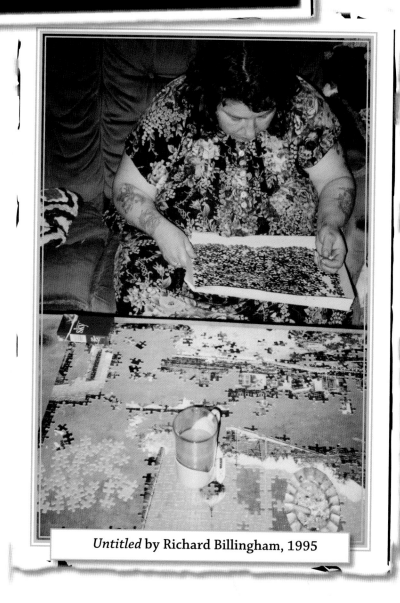

Untitled by Richard Billingham, 1995

We do not know the woman in this photograph either. We can see from the image that she enjoys doing jigsaw puzzles. We can make up a story about her life by looking at details in the picture. Her **tattoos** tell us what she might have been like when she was younger. We can see things on the floor and on the old sofa. This makes us think she is fairly poor.

Everyday lives

The British artist David Hockney took these snap shots of his mother on a day out together. It is a cold rainy day and his mother is wrapped up in waterproofs, sitting outside a ruined graveyard. The artist is trying to tell us several things. Firstly we can see that his mother is old. By showing her in a graveyard he could be thinking that she will die one day too. He took the photographs quickly and put them in a **collage**. The style of the finished image tells us about their relaxed and loving relationship.

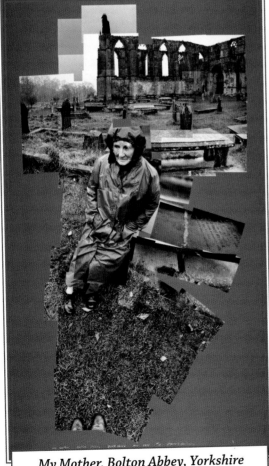

My Mother, Bolton Abbey, Yorkshire
by David Hockney, 1982

Looking at this photo we get the idea that the artist has a close relationship with his mother.

Polaroid cameras

Before digital cameras were invented, people had to wait for film to be developed before they could see a finished photograph. The Polaroid camera was good for taking quick snaps that were ready in minutes.

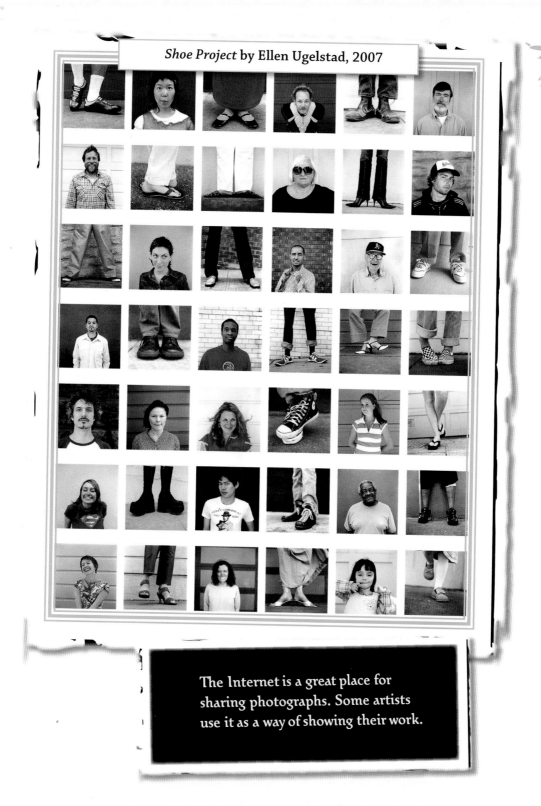

Shoe Project by Ellen Ugelstad, 2007

The Internet is a great place for sharing photographs. Some artists use it as a way of showing their work.

A Norwegian photographer took these pictures of people and their shoes. People have to wear shoes every day for practical reasons. This artist wanted to show that people can show us something about their personality with their shoes. She put the finished photographs on a website.

Photos inspired by paintings

This painting is by a Dutch artist called Vermeer. He was very famous for painting scenes of everyday life. We call these **genre paintings**. In this painting we see a young woman reading a letter in front of an open window. Does she look as though she is enjoying what she is reading? Look at her expression. What could be in the letter?

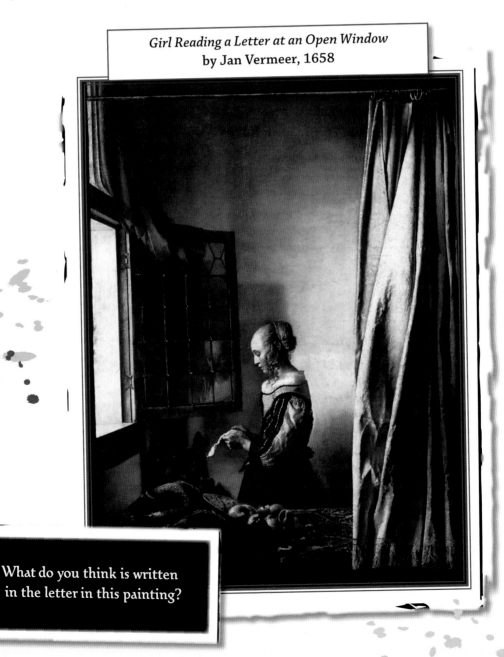

Girl Reading a Letter at an Open Window
by Jan Vermeer, 1658

What do you think is written
in the letter in this painting?

Think about it!

This photograph was taken over three hundred years after the painting was made. Look at both images carefully and see if you can spot the differences between them. How are they similar?

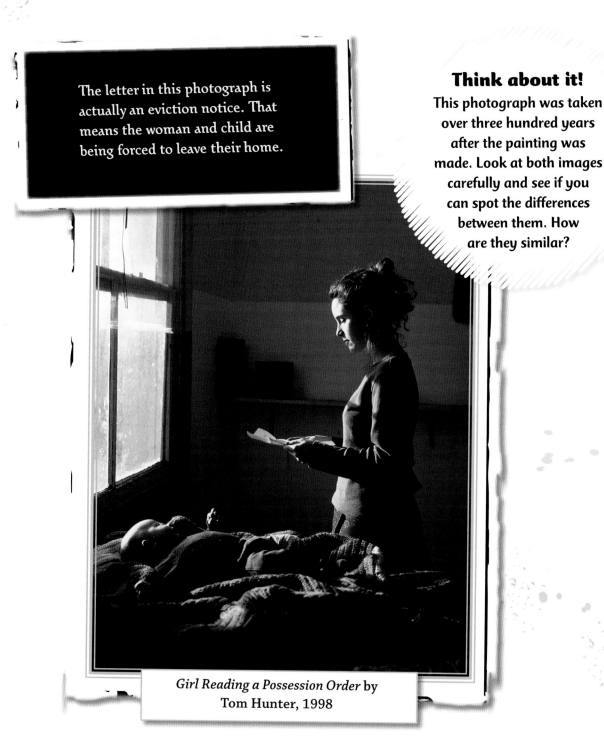

Girl Reading a Possession Order by Tom Hunter, 1998

This photograph is by the artist Tom Hunter. He has set up the same scene or **composition** but he has made it in modern day London. We can see a baby on a bed instead of fruit on the table. The young woman is now dressed in modern clothes and reading a letter in front of a closed window. Does she have the same expression as the Dutch woman in Vermeer's painting?

Celebrity

American **Pop artist** Andy Warhol believed that everyone could be famous for 15 minutes. Most of the people that he took photographs of were famous for a lot longer. He also made **screen-prints** of these celebrities. Warhol would pick a photograph and enlarge it to the size he wanted. He would then transfer it in glue onto the silk screen and roll ink across it. The result was a dramatic image with no wrinkles or lines in the face.

Marilyn Monroe by Andy Warhol, 1967 (detail)

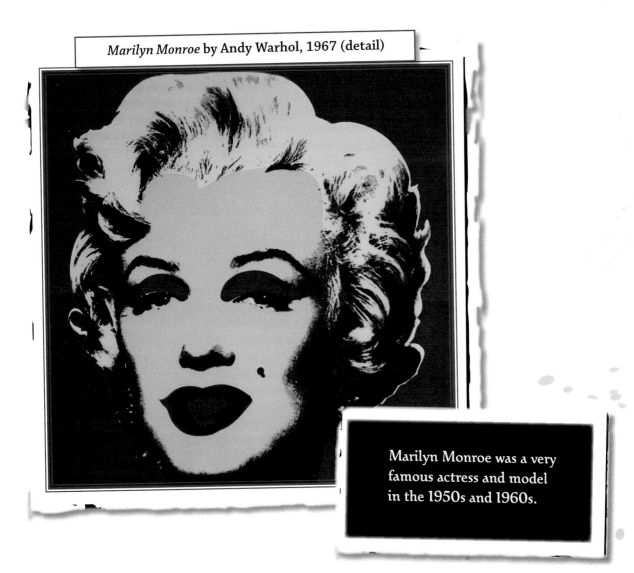

Marilyn Monroe was a very famous actress and model in the 1950s and 1960s.

This photograph shows the model, Twiggy. She became very famous after her picture was published all over the world.

Perfect

Today we see photographs of celebrities all the time. People use computers to change photographs so celebrities seem to look perfect.

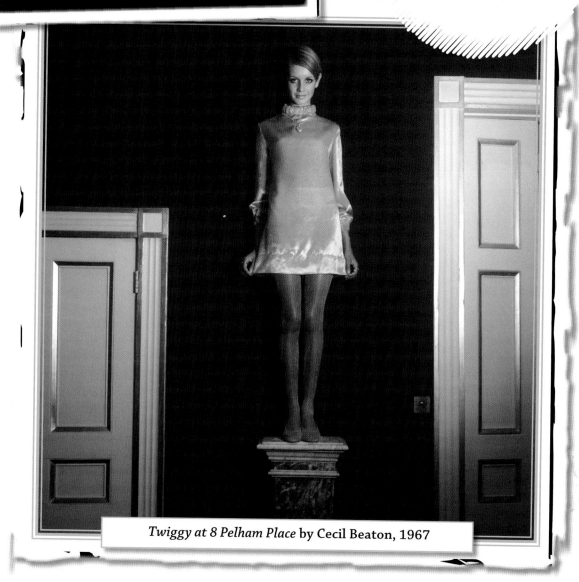

Twiggy at 8 Pelham Place by Cecil Beaton, 1967

A fashion photographer took this photograph for a magazine. Fashion photography is supposed to show clothes in a way that will make people want to buy them. Fashion photographs can make people think that buying certain clothes will give them a certain lifestyle. In this photograph the model looks like a beautiful statue.

Powerful images

This photograph was taken by one of the first people to land on the moon. The moment in history was so important that the photograph has become one of the most famous images of the 20th century. It shows an astronaut called Buzz Aldrin standing on the moon's surface. The photograph also includes the photographer, Neil Armstrong. You can see his reflection in Buzz's helmet visor. The camera had to be specially designed to work on the moon, where there is no **gravity**. It is an image that shows that humans are capable of incredible things.

Can you spot the astronauts' moon-landing craft, the *Eagle*, reflected in the visor?

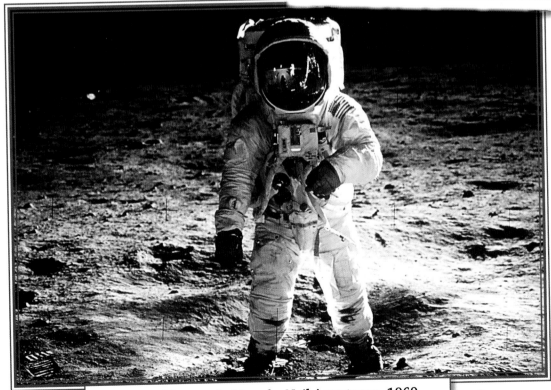

Buzz Aldrin on the Moon by Neil Armstrong, 1969

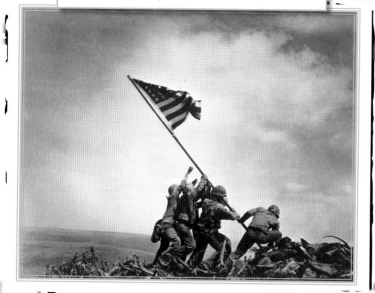

Iwo Jima by Joe Rosenthal, 1945

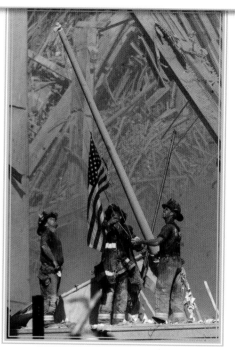

Firefighters at the World Trade Center by Thomas Franklin, 2001

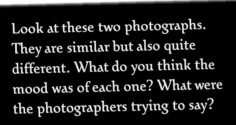

Look at these two photographs. They are similar but also quite different. What do you think the mood was of each one? What were the photographers trying to say?

Photographs with powerful messages

Here we see a group of soldiers at the end of World War II, raising the US flag on the Japanese island of Iwo Jima. The US had just beaten the Japanese. We can't see the men's faces so they represent all soldiers. The photograph could also have a more general message about the struggles of war. Another photographer used the same **composition** after the September 11 attacks on the USA in 2001. This time the soldiers were replaced by firefighters.

Things you can't normally see

It would normally be impossible for us to see the shape a drop of milk makes as it falls on a plate. Here the photographer has used a piece of lighting equipment called a **stroboscope**. In the photograph it looks as though time has stopped. The next droplet has already fallen and another splash is only a second away. The white milk stands out against the red plate, and this helps us see the image as clearly as possible. Edgerton also took photographs of bullets shooting in and out of soft materials.

The reflection on the shiny plate means we can also see underneath the splash of milk.

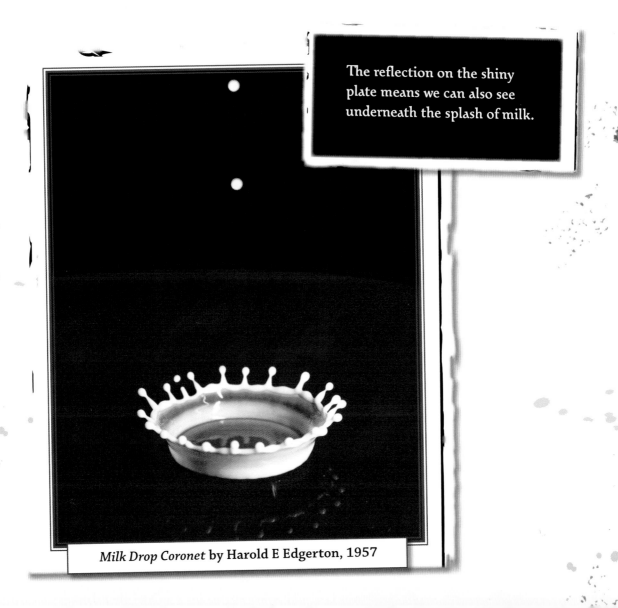

Milk Drop Coronet by Harold E Edgerton, 1957

Do you think the people
who live in this village would
recognize it in the photograph?

Home from the air

It may be possible to see
an aerial photograph of
the place you live on the
Internet with websites such
as Google Earth.

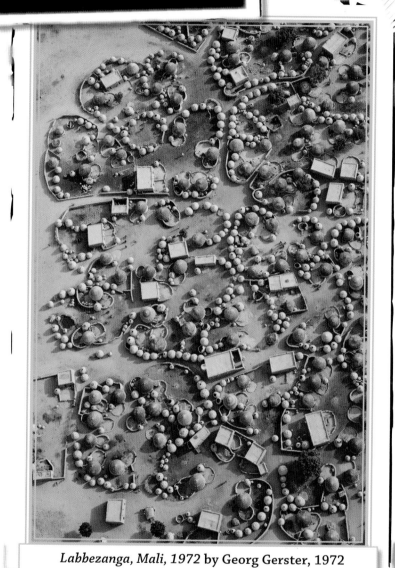

Labbezanga, Mali, 1972 by Georg Gerster, 1972

Georg Gerster takes many of his photographs from low-flying
planes. This is called **aerial** photography. Here we can see an aerial
shot of an African village. The roofs of the mud huts and the curved
walls between them look like beads strung together on strings. The
overall pattern is not something many people would have seen
before he took the photograph.

Capturing a moment

This photograph of children on a hot summer's day captures a special moment. When you look at this photograph you can see how much the children are enjoying themselves. You can almost feel how cold the spray of water is. The children's reactions are clear on their faces as they shout with joy, and maybe shock at the cold water. Compare this to the looks on the adults' faces. Do you think they want to join in too?

Summer, the Lower East Side by Weegee, 1937

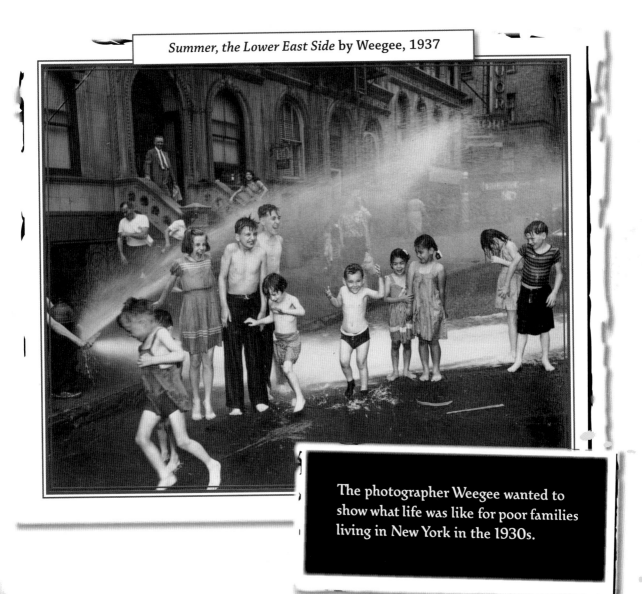

The photographer Weegee wanted to show what life was like for poor families living in New York in the 1930s.

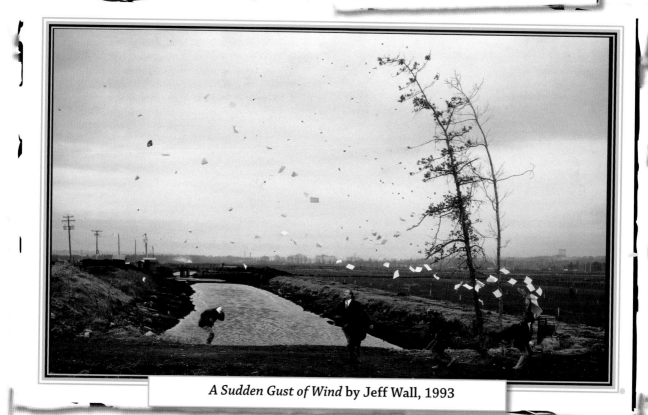

A Sudden Gust of Wind by Jeff Wall, 1993

Panic!

This photograph seems to capture a moment too. We can see people walking in the country by a river. One person is carrying a pile of papers when a sudden gust of wind lifts the papers from his hands and throws them into the air. The photograph has caught the movements of each person. Two people are trying to stay standing up in the wind. The man in the centre looks as if he wants to help catch the flying papers, but it looks hopeless. In fact, the photographer set up this scene using a group of actors.

Carefully set up photographs

This photograph was set up by the photographer to look unusual. The tears in this photograph are not real. We can tell this because they are perfectly round and there is no other mark on the model's face. When we cry, tears come out of tear ducts in our eyes. In this photograph there is no sign of where the tears have come from. In fact, these tears are made from glass. Tears are usually a sign of sadness or happiness, but in this photograph the model just stares upwards.

Tears by Man Ray, 1930

The photographer has zoomed in to just one feature on the model's face. This makes us look at it in more detail. Have you ever noticed how an eye glints, or the way eyelashes grow?

There is a famous artist called Salvador Dali in this amazing photograph. Today an artist could easily use digital technology to create a picture like this. However, this photograph was taken in 1948, before the technology was invented. The photographer had to use assistants who threw the water and cats across the scene as Dali jumped in the air. Other objects were held in the air by thread. The chair was held in position by Halsman's wife.

Dali Atomicus by Philippe Halsman, 1948

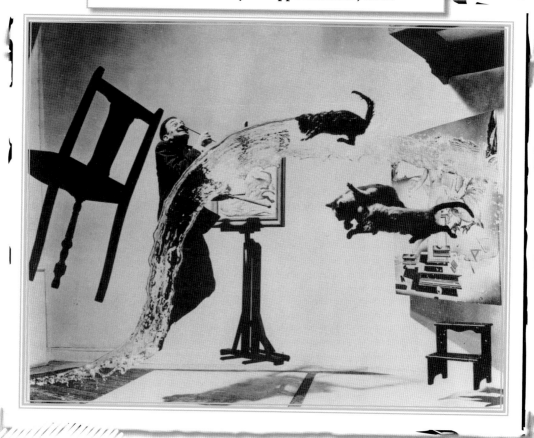

Dali

Salvador Dali (1904–1989) was the most famous Surrealist artist. Surrealists tried to realistically paint what might be seen in a dream. Dali's works, although very realistic, contained things you would never see in real life, such as melting clocks.

Philippe Halsman tried to photograph the type of scene that Dali would have painted. Did he succeed?

21

Altering images

Look closely at this photograph. Is it a cat or a person? It is actually two photographs. The artist started with a photograph of herself. Then she placed the cat image on top. This is a **negative** on transparent film, so we can see through to the photograph underneath. The final result is a rather creepy **self-portrait** of a 'cat woman'.

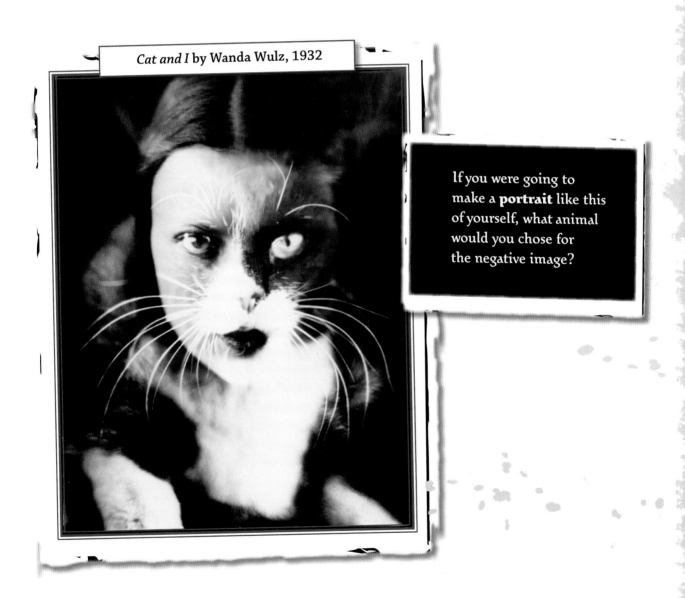

Cat and I by Wanda Wulz, 1932

If you were going to make a **portrait** like this of yourself, what animal would you chose for the negative image?

This funny photograph of sheep has been created using more modern technology. The artist has pasted red glowing eyes onto the animals using a computer. It makes the animals look like cartoon characters. Perhaps it also tells us how the artist feels walking through a field of sheep. Does he think they are all watching him?

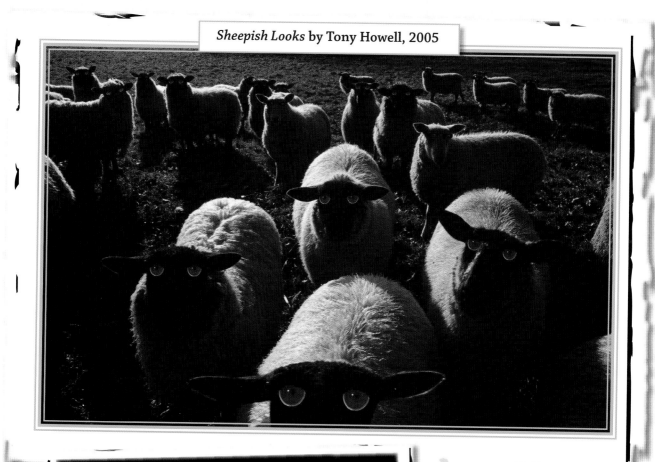

Sheepish Looks by Tony Howell, 2005

Tony Howell, who took the photograph of the sheep, is famous for his beautiful pictures of **landscapes** and flowers. Why do you think he made this image?

Photojournalism

When photographs are used to tell the news it is called photojournalism. Photographers have worked in this way since the 1920s. Andreas Feininger is the photojournalist who took this image. He has used his camera and skills to create a **self-portrait**. He has turned the camera on its side so the **lens** and **eye-piece** match the line of his eyes. The top of his camera disguises his nose. It is as though the camera has become part of the photographer.

> This picture shows that both the machine and the artist are needed to create photography.

The Photojournalist by Andreas Feininger, 1955

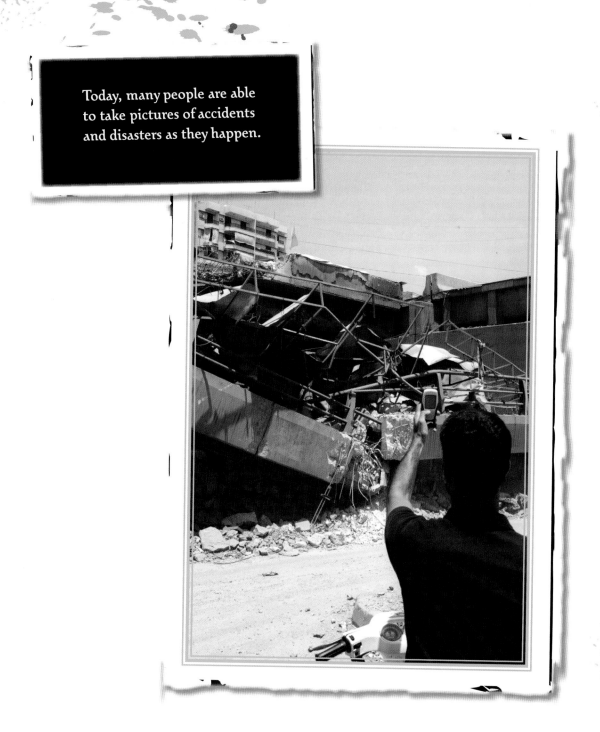

Today, many people are able to take pictures of accidents and disasters as they happen.

Today, many mobile phones have cameras. This means that many more people are able to try photojournalism. Television news stations and newspapers ask people to send in photographs and movies of big stories they see around them. Often non-professionals are there to take pictures before professional **journalists**. This means that we can now see the most extraordinary photographs of key historical events as they happen.

Moving pictures

In this book we have looked at the many reasons why people take photographs and how they produce their work. All have been still photographs capturing one moment in time. Today, we are also used to moving images on film and television.

One of the first examples of moving images used an instrument called a **zoetrope**. It worked by placing many photographs of a moving subject around the sides of a special wheel.

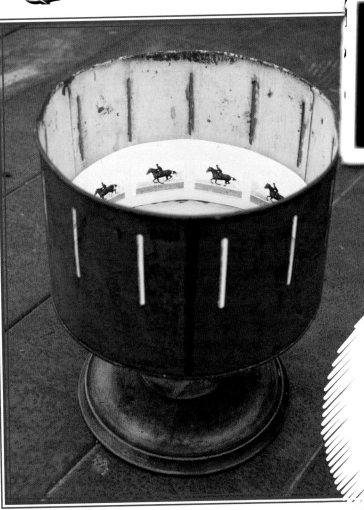

People would spin the wheel and look at the photographs through small viewing slits. They would see one moving image.

Did you know?

The zoetrope works in a similar way to a flick book. You can make one by drawing a simple picture in the corner of each page of a book. Make each drawing a little different from the last. Flick the pages quickly and the images seem to move. This is how animation used to work.

We call each photograph a **frame**.
When the frames are seen quickly
one after another, the images appear
to move.

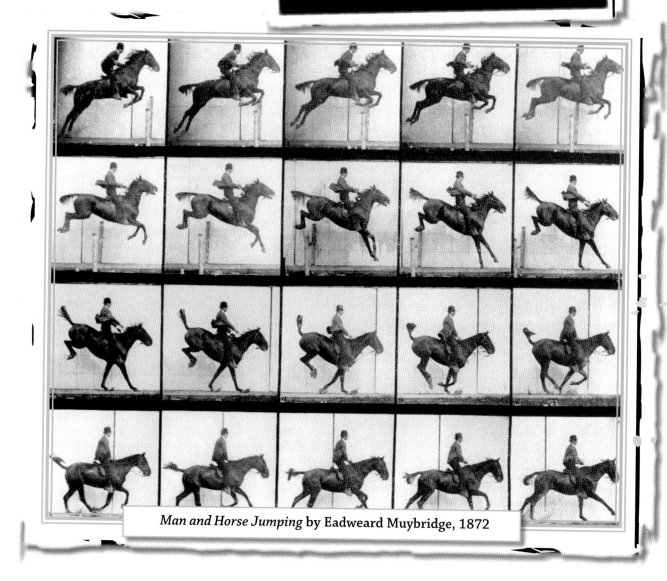

Man and Horse Jumping by Eadweard Muybridge, 1872

As technology changed it was possible for cameras to capture action
as it happened. Twelve cameras were used to take these photographs
of a horse jumping. Each camera was started by the last so that the
final shots look like they are moving when they are played in order.
Even with today's digital technology, this is the basic way that all
moving images work.

Timeline

Where to see photography

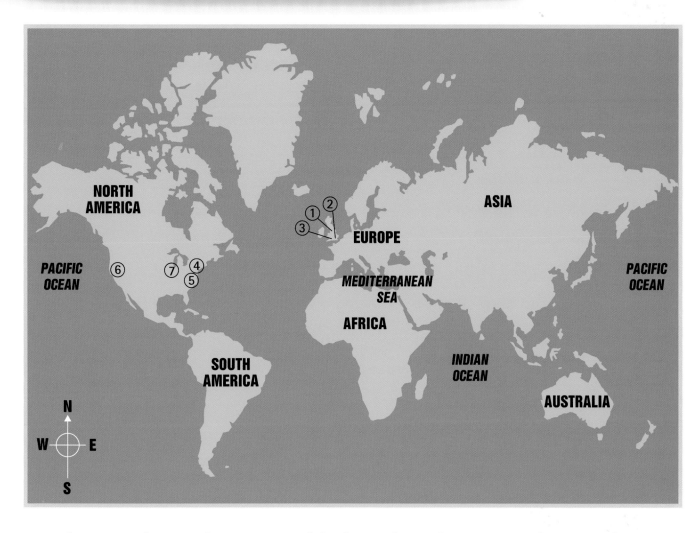

This map shows where some of the best places for viewing photography can be found.

① Bradford, UK
National Media
Museum

② London, UK
Victoria and
Albert Museum
National Portrait
Gallery

③ Wiltshire, UK
Fox Talbot Museum
of Photography

④ New York City, USA
The Metropolitan
Museum of Art
International Center
of Photography

⑤ Philadelphia,
USA The Franklin
Institute (history
of photography)

⑥ Los Angeles, USA
The Getty Center

⑦ Chicago, USA
Chicago Institute
of Art

Glossary

aerial seen from the air

animation series of pictures shown quickly so they look like a moving image

collage picture made up of lots of smaller pictures

composition how a painting, drawing or photograph is put together

eye-piece the part of a camera that the photographer looks through

frame small picture on a strip of film

genre painting painting showing a scene from everyday life

gravity force that holds us down on the Earth

journalists people who report news events

landscape picture of outdoor scenery

lens curved glass in a camera that focuses light from the subject

negative film that a photograph is first taken with

Pop artist belonging to a group of artists who used themes from popular culture in the 1950s and 1960s

portrait painting or photograph of a real person or animal

screen-print way of producing the same image many times

self-portrait an artist's picture of him or herself

stroboscope instrument used to make a moving object appear to be stationary

tattoos permanent designs made on the skin

zoetrope device that shows many small pictures very quickly so they look like a moving image

Learn more

Books to read

Photography (DK Eyewitness Guides), Alan Buckingham (Dorling Kindersley, 2004)

Surrealism (Art on the Wall), Richard Spilsbury (Heinemann Library, 2008)

Websites to visit

The National Portrait Gallery features a lot of photography.

www.npg.org.uk

The Tate Gallery kids website

www.tate.org.uk/kids

The Victoria and Albert Museum in London houses one of the largest collections of photography.

www.vam.ac.uk

Index